How to Write an Essay: A Beginner's Guide

Sean O'Neill

ISBN-13: 978-1530802449
ISBN-10: 153080244X

Special thanks to Kaila Herin,
Writing Tutoring Director
at Concordia University, Ann Arbor, MI
for her input and encouragement.

Table of Contents

Introduction

What is an essay? A pain in the neck? The bane of your existence? Yes, perhaps. But there comes a time in every student's life when the Mount Everest of essay-writing has to be climbed. According to one definition: an essay is a piece of writing that methodically analyzes and evaluates a topic or issue. Fundamentally, an essay is designed to get your academic opinion on a particular matter.

Generally what an instructor or teacher is looking for in your essay is some sign that a brain is lurking somewhere between your ears and that you haven't slept through all the lectures. Let's make the huge assumption for the moment that both statements are true. How do you go about the task of proving them to the teacher? Well, first of all, you have to read the materials that you have been steered towards during the course. Secondly – although this may seem obvious – you have to understand what you are reading. Thirdly, you have to write about what you've read in a convincing way.

There are four main types of essay that you might be asked to write: Argumentative, Expository, Descriptive, and Narrative. Each of them is approached in a different way and in the course of this book we will cover how to write each of them successfully. It goes without saying that you should ascertain from your teacher what kind of essay you have been assigned. Is it argumentative, expository, descriptive, or narrative? It is important to understand which of these is being required of you, because without that key piece of information you may write a brilliant essay, but still fail because you tackled it in the completely wrong way.

In this book we will cover everything that you need to know in order to successfully produce an essay out of thin air, which is on time and gets you as high a grade as possible.

Chapter 1 - The Expository Essay

What is an expository essay? Well, the word "expository" means explanatory. So in an expository essay you are attempting to explain something, and that something is contained in the teacher's essay assignment statement. It differs from the argumentative essay in that you are not being asked to make a case for or against anything, but simply to give an explanation. An expository essay is a type of essay that is often assigned as a paper to assess whether you have assimilated what the teacher has been talking about during class, or to find out if you know how to use the research material that has been suggested to you as background reading. It is sometimes called the "5-paragraph essay," but in reality the number of paragraphs is not important (unless the assignment stipulates a paragraph limit). Essentially, it is just an essay that is relatively short.

An expository essay, as with probably anything else you can think of, has a beginning, a middle and an end – or, better put, an introduction, a body and a conclusion. The introduction introduces the central idea you'll talk about in the essay. The main body presents evidence to back up the idea. This is the core of the essay and should be at least 3-4 paragraphs long. The conclusion simply sums up what you have said in the essay.

The sorts of essay assignments you might encounter are like the following:

- Explore how poverty can affect a country's productivity and economy.
- Describe how communication has changed in the past 20 years with particular reference to advances in

technology.

- What is your favorite technology business (Apple, Microsoft, IBM etc.)? How would you describe, in simple terms, how the business was started, what products it sells, how it makes money, and what are its main challenges.
- How does global warming affect western Europe, especially its impact on coastal cities.
- What were the direct and indirect causes of World War I?
- What is your favorite novel? Summarize and analyze its main features.

Before you begin, you should draw up a brief outline of what is going to be contained in your essay, showing briefly what each paragraph will contain. The reason for the outline is because the expository essay is supposed to follow a logical progression of thought from one paragraph to the next. If you don't draw up an outline you may end up with an essay that is disjointed, or turns out to be a jumble of thoughts and ideas put down in a haphazard way. That in turn will lower your grade for the paper.

The Introductory Paragraph

You usually need only one paragraph for the introduction and it should contain a clear and concise description of what you will be saying in the rest of the essay. It is usually a good idea in the first paragraph to start off speaking generally about the context of the subject and then focus in on the topic you are supposed to be writing about, as you will see from the examples below:

Explore how poverty can affect a country's productivity and economy.

There are many factors that can affect how productive a country can become. A wide variety of social, economic, and political elements plays into a nation's standing in the world and has a bearing on how it can maintain internal cohesiveness and provide a prosperous environment for its citizens in which to live and work. One of the factors that can impact a country's degree of success is the issue of poverty.

Describe how communication has changed in the past 20 years with particular reference to advances in technology.

One of the characteristics that separates human beings from animals, apart from self-awareness and the ability to walk upright, is their capacity for communicating with each other. This has had a huge impact on how human beings organize themselves and achieve what sometimes look like miraculous feats. In the past 20 years, technology has played a big part in how we communicate with each other, whether for good or ill. Let us examine its impact on our social lives and our work.

What were the direct and indirect causes of World War I?

World war I, or "The Great War," as it was referred to at the time, was a tragic event spanning the years 1914 to 1918 in which millions of men died in battle. In the aftermath, it was to change the way in which countries in Europe related to one another and also how individuals in society related to each other within those countries. The war came about as a result of many factors and in this essay I would like to examine some of the main ones and show how they contributed to the eventual conflict.

Each of these introductory paragraphs starts off with some general comments aimed at putting the subject into context. The paragraph then states what the rest of the essay is going to cover.

The Body of the Essay

There should be a clear transition between the introduction and the next paragraph. What that means is that you should pick up where the first paragraph left off, i.e. talking about the issue at hand. You should not go off at a tangent and talk about something completely different. The beginning of the body of the essay should expand on what you have just said at the end of the introduction, and the rest of the essay should lead on from that.

Each paragraph within the body of the essay should add to the description or explanation you are trying to get across. You can do this using a number of different techniques such as:

- Using examples to back up what you are trying to say.
- Showing cause and effect to illustrate what you mean.
- Comparing two or more things related to the subject and contrasting them with each other.

- Analyzing a process or function in order to describe in more detail how something works.
- Defining different words or functions in order to clarify what you are saying.

Each paragraph should be restricted to getting across only one point. When you have finished explaining that point, start a new paragraph to explain a further point, and so on.

Sometimes when you are given an assignment for an expository essay, the teacher expects you to complete it in class, or perhaps you have had little time for preparation. So you will not have any time or resources available to carry out research in the subject. In this case, you would not be expected to produce much evidence for what you say in the essay. If you do have time to prepare, or have research resources available you will be able to bring in factual, logical, statistical or anecdotal evidence to support the points you are making.

Remember that this type of essay is usually expected to be pretty short. There may even be a word limit, or a limit to the number of paragraphs you are allowed. So there is no point in going on at length about the subject or getting bogged down with only one aspect of it. The aim here is to produce a piece of writing that is concise, easy to read and says what you need to say with the minimum amount of words.

The Conclusion

Often, the conclusion is the part of the essay that students find most difficult to write. But in reality it should be the easiest. The reason for this is that you are saying nothing new in the concluding paragraph that you haven't already said in the body of the essay. In other words, the conclusion is not the place to introduce new information. So how do you write a conclusion? Well, you look at your introduction and briefly restate or paraphrase what you said there. Then you summarize what was said in the body of the essay, dedicating perhaps one sentence to each paragraph in the body. And lastly, you may add a concluding sentence summarizing the entire essay.

The concluding paragraph is the one that readers will take away from the essay. It is the part of the essay they are most likely to remember. So it should be brief and to the point. Try to cut out any extra information that is not really needed to get your point across.

There are a number of general issues involved in writing your essay, including your writing style, getting the paragraphing right and some common grammatical and punctuation errors. These are covered in chapter 5 and you should read through that chapter before embarking on your essay.

Chapter 2 - The Descriptive Essay

The descriptive essay is, basically, what it sounds like: an essay that describes something. You can be asked to describe a place, an object, an experience, an emotion, a situation, or a person. With this kind of essay the key is to be creative. The instructor or teacher is looking for something that will excite the imagination, something that will make your essay stand out from the crowd. For it to be successful, the essay has to explain the subject in as clear a way as possible so that the reader is in no doubt what you are describing.

Typical descriptive essay topics in an academic setting might be: in Art History: "Describe your experience of your first encounter with a particular school of painting;" or in Social Work: "Describe your experience of your internship at the home for the aged;" or in English Literature: "Describe the impact that one of Shakespeare's plays has had on you;" or in Foreign Language Studies: "Describe your first experience of conversing in a foreign language."

Once you have received the assignment, before you start to write, set aside a little time to brainstorm on the subject. For example, if the assignment asks you to describe your car, you might write down the color, the model and make, the shape, whether the seats are of cloth or leather, the engine size, the mileage on the odometer, the gas consumption, and so on. Then you can arrange your list moving from, say, general features to more specific elements. Brainstorming and coming up with a list helps you to organize your thoughts before you begin to write. In that way your essay will not just be a clutter of descriptive sentences, but a structured piece of writing that allows you to create as vivid a picture as possible in the mind of the reader.

For the descriptive essay you should try to use vivid and specific language: e.g. instead of writing the word "sheep," choose something more specific like "ram," "ewe," or "lamb." Instead of "field of grain," write "two-acre plot of land full of ripe barley." Instead of "angry," choose something more vivid like "outraged," "livid," or "infuriated."

Good descriptions, as much as possible, use the five senses to get across the meaning. What does the subject look like, smell like, sound like, feel like or even taste like?

Similarly it is a good idea to try to engage the emotions of the reader. If you are describing something personal, like bereavement, extreme joy, or indifference, then try to describe how that felt for you.

Use metaphor and simile to enhance your description.

What is a Metaphor?

A metaphor is a figure of speech in which a word or phrase is applied to an object or action to which it is not literally applicable. Examples are: "he sank into the pit of despair"; "she was on cloud nine with happiness"; "he was green with envy"; "her tongue was razor sharp". These examples are, of course, very familiar, if not hackneyed to death, and as a result not necessarily effective. A good essay will contain apt, but fresh, metaphors, not clichés.

What is a Simile?

A simile is a figure of speech involving the comparison of one thing with another thing of a different kind, used to make a description more emphatic or vivid. It usually employs the words "like" or "as". Examples are: "the clouds hunched over like a weightlifter's back," "his frown was as tight as a clenched fist," "the day dragged on like a turtle on weed."

Using metaphor and simile can add depth and originality to your essay, but try not to overuse them, otherwise the effect will seem forced and contrived.

One of your goals is to evoke a strong sense of familiarity and appreciation in the reader. If your reader can walk away from the essay craving the blueberry pie you just described, you are on your way to writing effective descriptive essays.

Some examples of opening paragraphs:

One describing a fishing trip.

I was awakened at 5.30 a.m. by Jack. He had been up and about for an hour or so. I was groggy and made my way out of the ramshackle bedroom to what we called the "living room" of the shack – although it too was ramshackle and smelled of mothballs and wood smoke. I rubbed the sleep from my eyes and staggered forward into the light of the oil lamp, like a newborn calf bleating for milk. The milk I poured from the glass bottle was half-gone and tasted sour. (There was no refrigerator.) I was a newborn in more than my craving for food. It took me about half an hour to fully waken up and by then Jack had packed all the gear: the fishing poles, the baits, the tackle and the sandwich lunch that would have to wait for four hours or so while we set off downriver and eventually reached the open waters of the lake ten miles below us as the crow flies. Eventually I rallied and shook myself into consciousness and we were off, two homing pigeons trained to fish from early childhood and headed home to the lake and the catch of salmon we had set our hearts on ever since last November when I had suggested the trip.

And one describing a visit to an art gallery.

Even before we had arrived at the Brera gallery we knew it would be a fantastic experience. We came by coach, supplied by the hotel, from the town of Treviglio, just east of Milan. It had rained in the night and the streets sparkled and shone, and there was a smell of lilacs in the air as though someone had doused the entire city with some kind of exotic air-freshener. The coach arrived just at opening time and we were almost the first visitors to line up at the entrance waiting to get in. In the foyer, a gaggle of tourists was clucking round the little kiosk, which was selling postcards and souvenirs. But the main attraction for us all was the Mantegna painting of the Dead Christ, which was one of the artworks that we had studied during art class.

There are a number of general issues involved in writing your essay, including your writing style, getting the paragraphing right and some common grammatical and punctuation errors. These are covered in chapter 5 and you should read through that chapter before embarking on your essay.

Chapter 3 - The Narrative Essay

A narrative essay usually follows a logical string of events from start to finish. Essentially, you are telling a story or writing a report on a series of events. Since you are writing a story it is essential to include all the usual elements that would be contained in a short story: a beginning, a middle and an end. But you could also include character description and development, setting, climax and plot.

The only time a narrative essay might not be written strictly like a story is if you are asked to write a book report. If the book is a novel, then there will certainly be an element of story to your essay. However, if you are reporting on a book of nonfiction, there may be no clear way to turn it into a story. In that case, what you will be providing is an informative narrative for the reader.

This is a common assignment in History, where you are asked to describe a series of historical events. Some examples might be: "Give an account of the development of cloth-weaving during the Industrial Revolution;" or "How did the Battle of Waterloo proceed?;" or "How did the transition between the Roman Republic and the Roman Empire come about?"

A narrative essay can also be a story written about a personal experience. Writing a narrative essay provides an opportunity to get to know and understand yourself better. One of the best ways to reveal who you are is to write about how you became aware of something, gained a new way of seeing the world, a new insight.

Your essay should have a clear purpose, which you should explain in the introductory paragraph. For example:

The purpose of this essay is to provide a narrative of the plot of the novel "Jane Eyre" by Charlotte Brontë.

And your essay should be written from a clear viewpoint. Sometimes that viewpoint will be that of the author of the story, sometimes you may choose to be more general and opt for a third person narrative. Whichever you choose, stick with that point of view throughout the entire essay.

In a similar way to the descriptive essay, if appropriate to the subject matter, try to use specific and vivid language, and bring all five senses into play as you go through your narration.

Lastly, make sure that your essay is well organized. Often the way it is organized will be dictated by the chronology of the events you are narrating, but sometimes (as in the case of the nonfiction book report) it will not be immediately clear how to organize your essay. Either way, it is worth taking some time, before you start, to brainstorm and draw up a list of the things you think should be included in the essay.

A couple of examples of opening paragraphs:

A personal narrative on a moving experience.

One of the most profound experiences of my life was visiting a hospice for the terminally ill. My father had warned me that it might be disturbing, but in the end it turned out to be deeply moving. The result was that I ended up volunteering to go there every week for a couple of hours to help out, visiting with the patients and helping serve lunch.

An essay narrating the plot of an adventure book.

In the book "The Thirty-nine Steps," by John Buchan, the protagonist, Richard Hannay finds himself caught up in a conspiracy that threatens to instigate a war in Europe and force the British government to take up arms against her enemies. This essay provides a summary of the plot.

Richard Hannay, bored with civilian life after a hectic time serving as an officer on the Western Front, resolves to leave England and seek his fortune if something exciting does not happen soon. As though it were a prophecy, life suddenly turns nasty as an unknown man is murdered in his apartment block, but not before spinning him an almost incredible yarn about spies and secret codes and the threat to European countries' delicate relationships. Before long, Hannay is on the run, as the murder suspect, from faceless enemies and begins a circuitous chase from the villains of the piece. Hannay holds vital information that must be conveyed to the government as soon as possible if disaster is to be averted.

There are a number of general issues involved in writing your essay, including your writing style, getting the paragraphing right and some common grammatical and punctuation errors. These are covered in chapter 5 and you should read through that chapter before embarking on your essay.

Chapter 4 - The Argumentative Essay

What is an argumentative essay? It's a piece of writing on a topic, for which you are required to carry out research and background reading in order to collect, generate and evaluate evidence. The purpose of the argumentative essay is to allow the student to take a stance on a particular issue and back up that position with evidence showing why he/she is right. An argumentative essay is often assigned at the end of a course and usually involves lengthy, detailed research. It is worth pointing out that, no matter how emotive the subject of the essay may be, your argument or discussion of a particular issue should be based on evidence and reasoning, not on emotion. In fact, your teacher may even assign you an essay and ask you to back up a position which is contrary to your own views. What is being tested is not whether you are right or not, but rather how well you tackle the process of systematic reasoning in support of a given premise. The argumentative essay is, more often than not, the longest essay type you can expect, therefore this chapter is longer than the others because it goes into detail about how to successfully write one.

It is important to discern what kind of essay you are being asked to write. For example, if you are tackling an argumentative essay, there is no point starting off by describing a personal experience you have had. That is not what is being asked for in an argumentative essay. Ask your teacher, if necessary, to confirm what kind of essay has been assigned.

When setting the essay question, your tutor, instructor or teacher will specify how long the essay should be. This can be expressed as a word count, a number of paragraphs, or a number of pages. Although the argumentative essay is often lengthier than the other types of essay, it can, in fact be anything from 2 pages right up to a dissertation-length piece of several thousand words, depending on the class, the topic, or the teacher. It is important to stick to the guidelines you have been given and not make it too short or too long.

The Assignment

So, what sorts of assignments might you encounter with an argumentative essay? Here are some examples of argumentative essay assignments:

- Was William Shakespeare a closet Roman Catholic?
- Did the assassination of Archduke Ferdinand cause the First World War?
- Does Reality TV Promote Dangerous Stereotypes?
- Who brought about the end of the USSR??
- What Is More Important: Our Privacy or National Security?
- Is Modern Culture Ruining Childhood?
- What were the chief instruments of papal government from 1050-1300? How do they represent the expansion of effective papal jurisdiction in this period?
- Constantine's conversion was insincere. Discuss.

As you can see, the assignment questions listed above invite the essay-writer to take a position regarding the issue. But whichever side you fall on, you must back up your position with evidence and research. The essay should be divided into three main parts: the introduction, the body of the essay, and the conclusion. The introduction should state what you intend to demonstrate by your essay. This is called the thesis. (It may be that the thesis statement is given to you as part of the assignment.) The body of the essay should make good on that promise by backing up the original thesis you mentioned in the introduction. The conclusion, should explain what you just did in the essay, by summarizing the thesis and how you showed that it was true.

There are other kinds of argumentative essay assignments. One other type of assignment will give you a list of background reading material and ask you to support one side of an argument or the other, backing it up with evidence using the articles or reports provided.

A Summary of the Method

Say you have been given an argumentative essay assignment. Where do you start? Well, here is a quick and dirty ten-step guide to how to produce an essay.

1. Carry out research: Gather together all your source materials and start to read them. As you read you will gain knowledge of the subject and gradually become an expert. While you are researching the topic take notes. Jot down any interesting quotes that you can use in your essay when it comes time to write it. Make sure that you also note down where each quote came from, including the name of the book, magazine or website and the page number if applicable.

2. Analyze what you have found: Now that you have a good knowledge base, start analyzing the arguments of the material you're reading. Clearly define the claims, write out the reasons, the evidence. Look for weaknesses of logic, and also strengths. Learning how to write an essay begins by learning how to analyze essays and books written by others.

3. Brainstorm for ideas: For your essay to be successful it will require insight of your own. Make a list of questions on the topic and try to answer them. Keep thinking till you come up with original insights to write about.

4. Draw up a thesis: Choose your best idea and write it down. Your thesis is the main point that your essay is making, summed up in a concise sentence that lets the reader know where you're going and why. It's practically impossible to write a good essay without a clear thesis.

5. Outline your essay: Write down an outline. The outline should list all the paragraphs in the essay with a short phrase or sentence explaining what each paragraph is about.

6. Write the Introduction: Now sit down and write the essay. The introduction should grab the reader's attention, set up the issue, and lead into your thesis statement. You might begin by stating what the opposite view to your thesis is, then lead into your thesis by saying “However, in this essay I intend to prove the opposite” or something like that.

7. Write the body of the essay: Each individual paragraph should be focused on a single idea that supports your thesis. Begin paragraphs with topic sentences, support assertions with evidence, and expound your ideas in the clearest, most sensible way you can.

8. Write the conclusion: Conclude your essay by repeating the thesis and showing how you backed it up with evidence throughout the course of the essay. End on some memorable thought, perhaps a quotation, or an interesting twist of logic, or some call to action.

9. Add a Works Cited (references) page listing the details of your sources.

10. Review and Edit: You're not done writing your essay until you've polished your language by correcting the grammar, making sentences flow, incorporating rhythm, emphasis, adjusting the formality, giving it a level-headed tone, and making other intuitive edits. Proofread until it reads just how you want it to sound.

So lets look more closely at each of these steps and examine what needs to happen for it to be accomplished successfully.

1. Carry out research

Assembling Your Reading Material

This involves doing background reading. It may be that your tutor or teacher has already given you a list of the prescribed reading for the essay. You may also need to use the notes you took down during lectures on the subject. But similarly, you might want to do your own research and discover background material on your own. That usually goes down well with the teacher because it – theoretically – shows that you are thinking for yourself and you may earn higher points for that.

Often, when you are reading a book it may make reference to some other book that is related to the subject.

You might already own the book, but most likely you won't. If not, take a note of the book that is mentioned and, if possible, borrow the book from a library. If you can't find the book you're looking for in a regular public library then university libraries usually have a deeper selection of books on specific subjects.

Failing that, if the book is so rare or esoteric that it is not even in the university library, you may be able to find a cheap second-hand copy from one of the many book retailers online, for example Amazon or Bookfinder (although, that's not really an option if you have only a few days before the essay deadline). In any case, part of the fun in writing a essays (Yay! I hear you shout) lies in ferreting out background detail that you can then use to add color to your text.

It is a good idea to keep a running list of thoughts as you go through the process of preparing. The thoughts may be things to follow up, illustrations that come to you, responses to others' arguments, and so on. As you make them, note anything relevant, e.g., the pages of the source you are refuting or calling on. Just write them down as you go, and don't try to make anything of them until you get to the stage of putting together your argument. Then you can review your notes and look for ways to expand or insert them – or maybe just eliminate them because they were ill-conceived or irrelevant.

Plagiarism

Another source of background material is the Internet. However, there may be a strong temptation just to copy and paste whole chunks of text from Wikipedia into your essay. Don't do that. Teachers are not as dumb as you think they are and may be quite familiar with the text you are using. If not, remember that if you can find the text on the Internet, so can the teacher. If your teacher finds out that you have plagiarized the text of your essay, you may end up not just with a lower grade, but a fail. So be careful not to copy a lot of text directly. The same goes for other sources such as books or magazines – you shouldn't just copy the text into your essay. You can of course quote small chunks of text from your sources and if you do that you should always make sure that you put the proper citation in a footnote (see section 7 of this chapter under Citation for how to cite correctly).

Plagiarism is taken very seriously by both high-school teachers and college professors or tutors. Your teacher is expecting you to show that you understand the source material and can discuss it in an essay. So instead of quoting large chunks of text from your sources – which shows that you have not really engaged with the material – what you should be aiming at is a reasoned discussion of the issues that the sources raise. If you can do that competently you will undoubtedly receive a high grade for your paper.

On a similar vein, it is also not a particularly brilliant ploy to simply paraphrase what some other author has to say on the subject without coming up with your own conclusions on it. The teacher is looking for what you have to say about the topic. So if you are going to use a secondary text, either quote from it directly (small snippets only) or merely refer to it in the course of your own explanation.

If you are an undergraduate, your essay should normally rely almost entirely on weighing, citing and comparing the arguments of others. Originality should come mainly from how you express yourself and perhaps from analyzing what others have written. At the undergraduates stage, and even for early graduates (say, at the start of a masters program), attempting originality is usually not so helpful. But your essay should show genuine understanding of what has been read and some ability to take on board the arguments that are presented, by analyzing, deploying, and comparing the thoughts of the secondary sources.

Research and Evidence

There are two types of research or evidence: firsthand and secondhand.

Firsthand evidence is evidence that you have come up with by yourself, such as interviews you have conducted, experiments you have carried out, surveys you have distributed, and anecdotal evidence. (Generally, it is not a good idea to include your own personal experience as part of your evidence unless it can be verified by another source.)

Secondhand evidence consists of background research in books, periodicals, websites, TV programs and documentary films.

Sometimes the background material will be given to you as part of the assignment. But, equally, you may have to come up with your own background reading. In that case, usually the instructor or teacher will provide a course reading list from which to choose your research. Whichever type of research you are conducting, whether first- or secondhand, what is important is that your sources be credible. In other words they must be trustworthy, accurate and reliable.

There are ways of finding out whether a source is credible.

The date: How recent is the research or evidence? Some fields of study change rapidly, such as information technology, and in that case you will want to find sources that are up to date. Other fields, such as history, are not so time-critical because the facts of the past are, generally speaking, static. The only differences you may find between recent and old historical evidence is the stance a particular author takes on an issue or event, or if new evidence has come to light that challenges the factual accuracy of what was generally thought to be bona fide historical data.

The author: is the evidence provided by someone who has a good reputation in their field? A credible source will use footnotes to cite which secondary sources they themselves have used to compile their report or article. You can look up any of these citations to see whether they are provided by reliable sources. This is also a good way of collecting your own list of background reading for your essay.

The acceptability of the evidence: One of the places you are most likely to find information on virtually any subject is the Internet. However, it is worth trying to find out how acceptable that source is for the teacher who will be grading your paper. Some readers of your essay may value peer-reviewed journals as the most credible sources. Others may prefer general sources such as magazines with a wider readership, such as The New York Times. Try to verify the author of whatever books and articles you use for your research, the same goes for Internet sources. Is the article on the website of a particular respected institution? Is the author a respected authority? Can you ascertain the date of the Internet article?

The author's motive: What is the author's purpose in writing about this topic. If the author is trying to present a balanced view, where, for example, he/she cites various different sides of an argument, then that evidence is credible. If, on the other hand, an author comes down firmly in one camp or another concerning a particular issue, then you need to be careful that you research doesn't originate from only one side of a debate. If that is the case, you need to research what other views there are on the particular matter.

2. Analyze what you have found

Taking Notes

As you browse through the material you have found as background reading you will want to take notes, so that you can remember what you have researched. Note-taking is more than simply repeating stuff you've found in a library book somewhere. If you want to add some value to your potential readers' experience, you need to also write down your own reflections on the facts as you present them, perhaps giving valuable insights into events or clearer descriptions of processes or people than the reader is likely to find elsewhere. This is what will make your essay stand out from its rivals and it is the unique perspective that you have that will bump your grade up and even make your essay enjoyable for the teacher to read.

So you begin by opening a word-processing file and then simply writing down notes as they occur to you. One thing that I have found useful is to write notes in the most complete and polished way possible. What I mean is write as though you were composing the final version of the text rather than scrappy bits and pieces that you will have to tidy up or rewrite later. Writing in a more polished way saves time and ensures you have a solid product when you have finished taking notes and come to assemble your essay later on.

The only exception to this is if the assignment requires you to interview somebody. During an interview it is impossible to write in a finished fashion, because people talk much faster than you can write. Even if you could write that fast, it probably wouldn't be that useful because people don't talk in finished sentences anyway. So one way or another you are going to have to go over the notes you take during an interview, tidy them up and rewrite them.

It is also useful, if you don't have enough time to flesh out your notes, to write "stubs" instead. A stub is a little note that takes the place of the finished paragraph or section, such as: "*Insert section on Winston Churchill's drinking habits,*" or "*Include details of the Marie Celeste findings*," or "*place Venn diagram graphic here*." It can be a good idea to write these in italics in your word-processing document to distinguish them from the surrounding text. When you have completed your notes, you can go back over what you have written and replace the stubs with the actual text or diagrams or illustrations that are supposed to be inserted there.

Organizing Your Material

As you go through your background reading, your quotes and even your interview notes, you should be taking notes on what you are finding. At that point there is no need to organize these notes into a coherent format. That comes next.

Once you have gathered together all your notes you should have a word-processing file containing a list of paragraphs on various different aspects of the subject. It is at this point that you begin to organize. Go through all the paragraphs and write beside each one a short description of the topic it talks about – or a unique and meaningful code that you devise to help you remember what each paragraph talks about. If you are using a word-processing file you may find it easier to convert your list of paragraphs into a table so that each cell in the table contains one paragraph. Then add a column to the right of your table, so that you have a table with two columns: the one on the left with your paragraphs and the one on the right for the little notes indicating what each paragraph is about.

You will find as you go through that a topic may be spoken about in several paragraphs, all of which may be in different parts of the manuscript. For example, your essay may be about the history of a soccer club, say Chicago Fire; you might find on page one of your manuscript that one of the paragraphs talks about a game between Chicago Fire and the New York Red Bulls in 2007. So you write beside it New York Red Bulls (or NYRB, which is shorter and more convenient, but still comprehensible). Later on in your notes, you may find another reference to the Red Bulls. Again you write NYRB beside that paragraph. As you go through the text you find three more places where you talk about Chicago Fire's relationship with the Red Bulls. You mark these too.

Once you have marked all the paragraphs, you may

decide to combine all the references to the NY Red Bulls into one section of the essay. And this is the way you treat all the other paragraphs. If the same theme turns up in multiple places, it may well be a sign that you should combine them under one section. So you then rearrange all your paragraphs so that you keep ones that are about the same subject together. Again, if you are using a word-processing file and you have converted your text to a two-column table, then all you need to do is sort the table on the second column. That will automatically group all the paragraphs together according to their subject matter.

If there are some paragraphs that are too few to form a section on their own, look for subjects that have a similar theme: perhaps you can combine two or even three of the smaller paragraphs and give them a section of their own.

On the other hand, if you find that there are ten paragraphs that have the same theme, then that may be too large to be one section. So, you might go through them and see whether you can subdivide them into smaller groups of paragraphs, then make sections out of those subdivisions.

If you have a section that only has, say, one paragraph, but doesn't logically fit in with any of the other subjects, then that may be a sign that you should either expand on that subject in order to flesh out the material into a section-size chunk, or perhaps even eliminate it completely.

Sorting Your Material

Here's how to sort out your notes into the appropriate sections. This method works well with fairly long essays with plenty of research, but might not be needed for shorter essays. So, I have written up all my notes on the Chicago Fire soccer team in a Microsoft Word file. The first thing I do is to convert the text to a table. I select all the text in the file, by clicking **ctrl-A** (if you're using a Mac, substitute the command key for ctrl), or by choosing **Select All** from the Edit menu. Next click on the **Table** menu, choose **Convert** from the drop-down list, then click on **Convert Text to Table**. Lastly, add a column to the right of the table. Move your cursor to the top-right of the table; the cursor will change to a down-arrow. **Right-click** and choose **Insert Columns** from the drop-down list. That will give you a two-column table, with the text on the left and an empty column on the right. (There may be different commands if you are using a different word-processor, or version.) Now go down the list of paragraphs and mark in the second column what the subject of each paragraph is. It should look something like this:

Text	**Subject**
Para 1	History
Para 2	Establishment
Para 3	History
Para 4	2007–2012
Para 5	2013–present
Para 6	Teams
Para 7	Teams
Para 8	Organization
Para 9	2013–present
Para 10	Player acquisition and salaries
Para 11	Stadiums
Para 12	Organization
Para 13	Team names
Para 14	Teams
Para 15	Establishment

As you can see from this list, there are several paragraphs that have the same subject. In order to organize these properly, all you need to do is sort the table on the second column and that will magically group all the paragraphs together according to their subject matter. (If you get it wrong first time you can always hit the **undo** button.)

To do that, choose **Sort** from the Table menu, and sort on Column 2.

The new table should look as follows:

Text	**Subject**
Para 4	2007–2012
Para 5	2013–present
Para 9	2013–present
Para 2	Establishment
Para 15	Establishment
Para 1	History
Para 3	History
Para 8	Organization
Para 12	Organization
Para 10	Player acquisition and salaries
Para 11	Stadiums
Para 13	Team names
Para 6	Teams
Para 7	Teams
Para 14	Teams

Rationalizing Sections

From this list it is clear that some of the subjects have several paragraphs and could be sections in their own right, For example "Teams" seems to take up more space than other subjects. Similarly, "Establishment", "History",

"2013-present" and "Organization" each have more paragraphs than most of the others, so we might consider making each of these a section in its own right - although, depending on the length of the notes, it may be possible to combine "Establishment" and "History" into the same section, since the subject matter is quite close. To the same extent, we may choose to combine "2007-2012" and "2013-present" since, again, they cover similar subject matter.

One of the other things that emerges from this exercise is that some subjects seem to have very few paragraphs devoted to them – for example, "Player acquisition and salaries" and "Stadiums." So this may be a sign that we need to go back and do more research in those areas in order to expand each of these subjects into a section-length segment.

It is worth noting that once you have separated out your material into sections, you may need to do some final tweaking within each section itself. For instance, in the above example the section containing "History" might not be in chronological order, so you may need to rearrange the paragraphs within that section to avoid non-sequiturs.

It may also be the case that once you have bolted paragraphs together within a section, the text does not flow easily from one paragraph to the next. In that case, you will probably have to add linking phrases such as "Furthermore…," "It stands to reason, therefore…," or, "Because of this…." at the beginning of some paragraphs.

Beginning, Middle and End

Once you have reorganized your notes into sections, you then need to reposition those sections so that introductory material comes at the beginning of the essay, and concluding material comes at the end, with all the rest in logical order in the middle. For example, if we look at the list, we see that the segments are in ascending alphabetical order because we sorted it like that. But we may well decide to alter that order. For example, it seems logical that "Establishment" and "History" should come at the start of the essay. We may then decide that the style of the essay should follow a progression from general information to specific. So, perhaps the section on "History" could be followed by sections covering "2007-present," then "Organization." Both of which are more general than "Teams" and "Team Names".

None of the sections look as if they should come at the end of the essay. So that tells you that you need to write a concluding section summing up what has been covered in the course of the essay and drawing some conclusions.

3. Brainstorm for ideas

The next thing you need to do is to review your notes. Are they complete? Do they cover all the main aspects of the subject? Are any themes emerging already from the notes that could be useful when you come to actually write the essay? Are there any conflicting views on the subject? If so, it would be a good idea to include a discussion of these different standpoints in your essay.

As part of the brainstorming process, you should also be thinking about a possible structure for the essay. Should it be in chronological order? Should it move from general considerations to more specific matters? Should it begin with the main points of contention? Or should you introduce the subject stating what most people agree on?

4. Draw up a thesis

The thesis will be included in the introduction and it basically sets out the main point that you will be attempting to prove in the course of the essay. You may formulate it as a sentence beginning: "In this essay I will make the case that…," or something similar. See the section on writing the introduction for more details on the thesis statement and how to embed it in the introductory paragraph(s).

Sometimes the teacher or instructor will give you a ready-made thesis statement for you to use as the basis of your essay. If not, then you will have to come up with one yourself. As you were going through your research and taking notes of the various aspects of the subject and what the varying opinions were, you should have already been forming your own views on the topic. The thesis statement simply articulates the conclusion you have come to in as clear a way as possible on the basis of the facts you have researched and the different sides to the argument you have encountered.

5. Outline your essay

An outline is a document you write up that shows what is conveyed in each section of your essay. You could view it as a kind of extended table of contents, with a sentence under each section saying what you hope to get across in that section. From the work you have already done organizing your notes and brainstorming, you should already have a good idea what the layout of your essay will look like. The outline merely crystallizes that by showing the structure you will use to work through the material and get your point across.

The outline should show how you will progress your argument from one point to the next, where you will bring in views that oppose your own position, and how you will counter those claims. It is worth playing around with your outline to come up with the best structure that shows a logical progression from the introduction, through the body of the essay, to the conclusion.

The following shows how to structure your essay in such a way that you do justice to the research you have conducted and allows you to provide a well-thought-out outline that you can work from as you write the essay. The elements listed below should all be present in your argumentative essay.

How to present your argument

The general structure of the argument in your essay should be like this:
Claim – the statement telling the reader what case you intend to make in your essay. This will always come in the introductory paragraph.
Data: the evidence you have researched to support your claim.
Warrant: this is an explanation of how your data supports your claim.
Backing: any further reasoning or logical thought development that will support your claim.
Counterclaim: a claim that disagrees with your own claim. This will involve outlining contrary views to your own.
Rebuttal: Evidence you have gathered which disagrees with the counterclaim.

6. Write the Introduction

The introductory paragraph is, naturally, the first

thing your tutor will read when they pick up your essay. So it is important that your introductory paragraph(s) be strong, clear and concise.

The introductory paragraph should start by putting the issue in context. This may involve making some general comments before stating the "thesis." The thesis is where you state what you are aiming to achieve by the essay. The statement needs to be debatable. In other words, if your thesis statement is either too broad or it is something that nobody would really disagree with then you have a poor thesis statement. An example of thesis statements that are poor might be:

Pollution is bad for the environment.

Drug use is detrimental to society.

Slavery is wrong.

These statements are either too general or not really debatable since most rational people would agree with them. The thesis statement needs to be narrow in order to work well as the premise for your essay. It also needs to be specific enough so that you might reasonably suppose that people might disagree on it. For example:

America's anti-pollution efforts should focus on privately-owned cars.

Illegal drug use is detrimental because it encourages gang violence.

Slavery should be abolished in India, not because it is morally wrong, or illegal, but because slaves have a lower cost-benefit than paid workers.

Here are some examples of the opening paragraphs of some argumentative essays:

How Important Is Arts Education?

Nowadays, great emphasis is placed on the sciences and on the practical application of education to what is called "real life." This has resulted in an overbalance of education away from the traditional classical or humanities subjects to subjects that are deemed to be of practical value in securing a job once the student has left full-time education. This utilitarian approach has meant that subjects that do not appear to have a practical application are undervalued. However, in this essay I aim to prove that an arts education still has relevance and provides a valuable contribution to society in general and to the individual student in particular.

Is Modern Culture Ruining Childhood?

There are many advances in the fields of medicine, technology and engineering that provide great benefits to society. Whether it be the availability of information on the Internet, the ease of communication, by cell phone, text or email, or the complex mechanisms involved in running a car, these are all ways in which modern culture can contribute to making life easier to navigate for the individual member of society. However, there are also drawbacks in modern culture, especially for children, and in this essay I propose an alternative view, in which modern culture can be said to be responsible for ruining the childhoods of many members of society.

How relevant is God to the world of today?

Since the distant past, human beings have felt the need to seek meaning for their lives outside of themselves. The urge to validate existence in this way has caused the rise of many religions. In today's world, is it possible to get by without the need to worship a God? Many would say yes, that mankind has reached a level of sophistication and society has advanced sufficiently that God has become an irrelevance. However, in this essay I intend to make the case that humanity needs God more than ever and that far from being irrelevant, God is the answer to many problems that we face in our day-to-day lives.

It is evident from these three samples that not only does the introductory paragraph put the issue in context, but it also puts forward a contrasting view, before stating what the thesis of the essay will be. This makes the introduction balanced and reflects the logical way in which the essay will unfold from now on.

7. Write the body of the essay

Each paragraph in the body of the essay should be restricted to discussing only one point. If you find yourself tempted to bring in other points, then start a new paragraph. In addition, each paragraph should have a logical connection to the thesis statement you made in the introduction.

Just like in the introduction, in each paragraph, it is a good idea to present a contrasting view to the position you are taking before putting your own side of the argument. In the three examples above, the thesis statement begins with "However...," but we might as well have written "On the other hand...," "In contrast to that view...," or "Nevertheless...." What is required is a linking phrase that shows the contrast between what has been suggested and what you are about to say. This makes it easier for the reader to follow your train of thought and makes it clear what stance you are taking on the issue.

Another way of tackling this is to present contrary views in the first two or three paragraphs in the body of the essay; next spend some paragraphs showing how those opinions are faulty; and lastly go on to express your own views supported by evidence. It is not good practice to say that the contrary views are simply wrong. Instead, a better way of approaching contrasting opinions is to show how they may be based on inaccurate data, or state that times have changed and they are no longer relevant, or counter them by stating that they are based on an emotional response rather than on the evidence. You will score higher grades for putting forward a reasoned argument in this way.

In the body of the essay, you will be presenting your view backed up by evidence you have gathered through researching the subject. So it is important when you make a statement, that you can support what you are saying using your research, but you must also show how and why the evidence supports your view.

The evidence you gather to support your thesis

might be based on facts or events you have researched, or might be a logical argument showing how your thesis statement is correct, or might be based on statistics, or might be anecdotal evidence from which you extrapolate a general truth. You can use some or all of these to back up your thesis, but whichever you choose you must show that what you say is well researched, accurate, detailed and up to date. As mentioned, you should state what other sources are saying on the topic which do not necessarily tie in with your thesis statement. In fact, if there are contrary views, it would even be unethical not to mention them somewhere.

Here are a examples of paragraphs from the main bodies of a couple of argumentative essays:

In addition to this, many people who are involved in traditional publishing maintain that the reading public needs "gatekeepers" to vet what is published so that there is some level of quality control before a book gets into print. However, this argument does not hold up in today's publishing markets. One reason is that the reading public has online book retailers, for example, Amazon, where many books have been reviewed by readers already and their reviews and "star ratings" are shown right there along with the books' listing on websites selling books. It is true that there are a lot of low quality books that are published independently, but most members of the reading public simply do not buy them if they receive poor reviews. This level of self-regulation eradicates the need for publishers to act as gatekeepers and is a better gauge of book quality than a publisher's recommendation.

For centuries the system for purchasing artwork

meant that artists had to go to an art dealer, convince the gallery to sell whatever paintings were on offer and then wait, sometimes for weeks or months, before a sale was forthcoming. Even then, the dealer often took anything up to 50% of the profit from the sale. With the expense involved in buying art supplies, matting and framing the finished work, not to mention traveling costs and transportation, the artist generally fared poorly and often never made enough money to survive on. Nowadays, however, any fledgling artist can rustle up a website for a fairly modest outlay and advertise his or her work there. Also, online auction websites such as EBay provide a ready made marketplace to buy and sell artwork, thus cutting out the middlemen – the art dealer and the gallery – completely, which means that the artist can pocket 100% of the profit from each sale.

As you can see, each of these paragraphs shows a contrasting view to the point the author is trying to get across, before putting forward the author's own view, which is itself linked to the thesis statement made in the introduction.

In the first example, the views of traditional publishers are given an airing, but are then countered from the point of view of the author who chooses to publish independently.

In the second, the centuries-old system of selling artwork is contrasted with the modern facilities available to artists with which they can sell their artwork online.

If you have made your notes as polished as possible and have included your own thoughts on the subject in your notes, then there is a good chance that you will be able to copy and paste from them directly into your essay. That at least will give you a decent amount of material to work with. You will obviously have to make adjustments here and there to the notes that you include in your essay, but that is still better than starting from scratch.

Footnotes/Endnotes

As you write your essay, you will be quoting from various sources. When you do quote a source it is essential that you provide footnotes or endnotes that state where you got the information. Footnotes should appear at the bottom of the page your quote ended on and should be numbered sequentially. Your word processor will have a function that allows you to insert a footnote anywhere in the document. This feature automatically places a number next to the text in the body of the document and a footnote at the bottom of the page that the quote ends on. Similarly, your word processor will have a facility for inserting endnotes at the end of your document. Again, the program will allocate a number to each endnote automatically.

The advantage of footnotes, of course, is that the reader doesn't have to go searching through the list of citations that would appear at the end of the essay, because it's right there at the bottom of the page. On the other hand, footnotes can be a distraction, especially if you have more than one or two on a page, so you may opt for endnotes. Whichever you choose, it is important that you cite your source material properly using the style guide that is employed by the institution you are enrolled in or that the teacher has stipulated. Some common methods of citing external sources are shown in the next section.

You should always ask your teacher for guidance on whether footnotes or endnotes are more acceptable for their course. This may vary from one teacher to the other so it is worth checking this with each one.

Citation

When you quote or paraphrase or make reference to an external source you should say where that quote came from. This is called citation. There are three main styles used for citing external works that are mentioned in your essay: APA (American Psychological Association) Style, MLA (Modern Language Association) and the Chicago Manual of Style. One thing you need to do is find out from your teacher or instructor which method is used in their particular institution. APA is most commonly used by the Social Sciences disciplines, such as Psychology, Linguistics, Sociology, Economics, and Criminology, by Business and also by Nursing. MLA is normally used by English Studies, both Language and Literature, by Foreign Language and Literatures, Literary Criticism, Comparative Literature, and Cultural Studies. The Chicago Manual of Style is generally used in the fields of Literature, History, and the Arts. (It is sometimes used by the social sciences also.)

When citing a work that you have used for background research here is a summary of how it is done under each of the styles.

APA

Citations embedded in the text itself:

When using APA format for in-text citation, the author's last name and the year of publication for the source should appear after the text, for example, (Smith, 1998), and a complete reference should appear in the reference list at the end of the paper.

If you are referring to an idea from another work but not directly quoting the material, or making reference to an entire book, article or other work, you only have to make reference to the author and year of publication and not the page number in your in-text reference. All sources that are cited in the text must appear in the bibliography list at the end of the paper.

APA style requires authors to use the past tense or present perfect tense when using phrases to describe earlier research, for example, Smith (1988) **found**..., or Smith (1988) **has noted**...

Footnote or endnote citation: If you are citing a book, use this format:

Author last name, author first name. (Year of Publication). Title of work. Publisher City, State: Publisher, page(s).

If you are citing a magazine, use this format:

Author last name, author first name. (Year, month of Publication). Article title. Magazine Title, Volume(Issue), page(s).

More information on how to cite using APA, including citations for newspapers, websites, journals, films, and encyclopedias can be found in section 9 of this chapter, "Add a List of References".

MLA

Citations embedded in the text itself.

Here you have a choice, as follows:

Human beings have been described by Kenneth Burke as "symbol-using animals" (3).

OR Human beings have been described as "symbol-using animals" (Burke 3)

Both citations in the examples above, (3) and (Burke 3), tell readers that the information in the sentence can be located on page 3 of a work by an author named Burke. If readers want more information about this source, they can turn to the Works Cited page, where, under the name of Burke, they would find the following information:

Burke, Kenneth. Language as Symbolic Action: Essays on Life, Literature, and Method. Berkeley: U of California P, 1966. Print.

Footnote and endnote citation:

If you are citing a book, use this format:

Last Name, First Name. Book Title. Publisher City: Publisher Name, Year Published. Medium, page(s).

If you are citing a magazine, use this format:

Last Name, First Name. "Article Title." Magazine Name Publication Date: Page Numbers. Medium, page(s).

More information on how to cite using MLA, including citations for newspapers, websites, journals, films, and encyclopedias can be found in section 9 of this chapter, "Add a List of References".

The Chicago Manual of Style

Citations embedded in the text itself:

When using The Chicago style the format for in-text citation, the author's last name and the year of publication for the source should appear after the text, along with the page numbers, if available. For example, (Smith, 1998,

245), and a complete reference should appear in the bibliography at the end of the paper.

Footnote and endnote citation:

If you are citing a book, use this format:

Last Name, First Name. Title of Book. Publisher City: Publisher Name, Year Published, page(s).

If you are citing a magazine, use this format:

Last Name, First Name. Article title. Magazine Title, Month Date, Year of publication, page(s).

More information on how to cite using the Chicago Manual of Style, including citations for newspapers, websites, journals, films, and encyclopedias can be found in section 9 of this chapter, "Add a List of References".

Avoiding Logical Fallacies

As you go through your essay you will be building a case that supports your thesis statement. However, there are a number of logical errors you might fall foul of if you don't take care. Here are a few of the most common ones.

Wild connections: This is a form of argument in which we say if "A" is true, then eventually "Z" will be true, while missing out the intervening steps, "B" through "Y." An example might be: *A particular store banned guns on the premises. With that attitude, eventually guns will be banned everywhere. So we should never ban guns in stores.*

Wild generalizations: This involves drawing a conclusion before you have sufficient evidence. An example might be: *Even though it's only the first day, I can* *tell this is going to be a boring job.*

Non sequitur: This involves drawing a conclusion on the basis of a link where no link necessarily exists. An example might be: *I ate a peach and now I am sick. So the peach must have made me sick.*

Ad hominem: This seeks to discredit an opposing view by attacking the person who is proposing it. An example might be. *Bill Clinton committed adultery, therefore no one could trust his foreign policies.*

The above are just some of the logical pitfalls you can end up in. In order to avoid them, make sure that you work out your logical argument beforehand and that what you are saying is reasonable. To do this, challenge every statement you make in your essay and see whether it stands up to scrutiny as a valid argument.

8. Write the conclusion

The conclusion is where you wrap up the points you have made and draw the essay to a close. Students often find the conclusion difficult to write, but in fact it can be the easiest part of the essay. The conclusion is really the part of the essay that will remain with the reader and so it should be like a highly condensed version of the essay itself.

The conclusion should re-present the thesis or the stance you took in the introduction. But it shouldn't just restate it. The job of the conclusion is to readdress the thesis statement in the light of the evidence that has been presented throughout the essay.

The conclusion is not the place to introduce new information or points that you wish to make. If you still have something you want to say on the subject, add a paragraph to the body of the essay instead.

The conclusion, essentially, is a summary of what you have said in the essay. Restate why the topic is important, review the main points and review your thesis. You might also want to suggest further research that could be conducted in the light of your essay or research.

Here are some examples of concluding paragraphs:

As we have seen in this essay the arguments for retaining the British monarchy do not hold up under close scrutiny. It is true that in the past the monarchy provided the moral backbone of the country, but given the behavior of many of the royals, as displayed daily in the tabloid press, they now provide a poor example of how to live one's life. Again, some say that the royals provide the valuable service of representing the United Kingdom abroad. However, if we weigh that up against the expense of maintaining them in the lifestyle to which they have become accustomed, the cost is too great. For these and the other reasons set forth in this essay, it is clear that the institution of the monarchy should be abolished.

The cost of holding prisoners who have been convicted of crimes is staggering. If the punishment for a crime is supposed to be in some way redemptive or at least reformative so that the person no longer commits crimes, then it fails completely since it is a well-known fact that prisons are, more or less, a school for crime. Both of these drawbacks could be address by decriminalizing petty crimes and having more convicted criminals pay back to society by undertaking community services of various kinds, such as digging roads and other construction work. These are just some of the measures that would help to decrease the cost of the prison system and also contribute towards reforming criminals.

Each of these examples looks like a mini-essay in itself. That is because each of them is a summary of what was said in the body of the essay. Each example moves from point to point covering the main issues discussed in the preceding paragraphs. And each of them ends with a sentence that sums up the thesis position.

9. Add a List of References

In the course of preparing for your essay you may have had to consult various sources. As you carry out your research you should take a note of every book, magazine, documentary or interview you have used. When you have finished writing your essay it is standard practice to include a bibliography page (sometimes called a list of references, or list of works cited) at the end of the paper.

Again, there are rules that govern how you show this, depending on what style guide you use (APA, MLA, or Chicago Manual of Style). No matter what bibliography style you are using, the list should be in alphabetical order.

An APA list of references should be entitled "References." An MLA list of references should be entitled "Works Cited." A Chicago Manual of Style list of references should be entitled "Bibliography."

Here is a guide to how to cite some of the most common types of reference works that you may have consulted as you wrote your essay, including books, periodicals and websites. (NB. Where an item is italicized you should also italicize. In some cases only the initial capital in a title is capitalized. Also, where you see periods or commas inserted, do likewise.)

APA

References

Citing a book in print

Format:

Author last name, author initial. (Year of Publication). *Title of work.* Publisher City, State: Publisher.

Example:

Jumper, J. (1970). *How to kill time*. New York, NY: Bleep and Booster.

Citing a magazine article in print

Format:

Author last name, author initial. (Year, month of Publication). Article title. *Magazine Title, Volume* (Issue), pp.-pp.

Example:

Crum, K. (2006, April). Why I wear perfume. *Timecast, 167*(15), 3-40.

Citing a newspaper article in print

Format:

Author last name, author initial. (Year, Month Date of Publication). Article title. *Magazine Title*, p. page #.

Example:

Blighty, G. (2003, March 1). Why sheep are beginning to talk. *The York Chronicle*, p. D5.

Citing a general website article with an author

Format:

Author last name, author initial. (Year, Month Date of Publication). Article title. Retrieved from URL

Example:

Munster, B. (2014, January 19). The last dance saloon. Retrieved from http://the-last-dance-saloon

(If no author name is specified then simply omit it)

Citing a journal article in print

Format:

Author last name, author initial. (Publication Year). Article title. *Periodical Title, Volume*(Issue), pp.-pp.

Example:

Nevin, A. (1990). Pygmies in the outback. *The Pygmy Journal of the Hinterlands, 13*(3-4), 147-148.

Citing a film/Citing a movie

Format:

Producer last name, producer initial. (Producer), & Director last name, director initial. (Director). (Release Year). *Title of motion picture* [Motion Picture]. Country of Origin: Studio

Example:

Bunce, L. (Producer), & Solburger, W. (Director). (1994). *Gulp friction* [Motion Picture]. United States: Miraman.

Citing an encyclopedia entry in print

Format:

Author last name, author initial. (Publication Year). Entry title. In *Encyclopedia title*, (Vol. XX, pp. XX).City, State of publication: Publisher.

Example:

Smith, C., & Jones, A.H. (2012). Multiple personality disorder. In *Encyclopedia of psychology findings*. (Vol. 3, pp. 363-364) Lanham, MD: AltaMira Press.

MLA

Works Cited

Citing a book in print

Format:

Author last name, Author first name. *Book Title*. Publisher City: Publisher Name, Year Published. Medium.

Example:

Cavaglione, Giovanni. *Hairbrush technology*. Lansing: Shyster, 2003. Print.

Citing a magazine article in print

Format:

Author last name, Author first name. "Article Title." *Magazine Name* Publication Date: Page Numbers. Medium.

Example:

Fragonard, Jean. "Jones sees a mouse." *Timescale* Mar. 21 2008: 21-23. Print.

Citing a newspaper article in print

Format:

Author last name, Author first name. "Article Title." *Newspaper Name* Publication Date: Page Numbers. Medium.

Example:

Calvados, Miguel. "Spartans win again." *Lansing Gazette* Feb. 28 2003: 4-6. Print.

Citing a general website article with an author

Format:

Author last name, Author first name. "Page Title." *Website Title*. Sponsoring Institution/Publisher. Publication Date: Page Numbers. Medium.

Example:

Jones, Steve. "Eisenhower inaugurated as President." *ACBRT.com*. A Chronic Battle Right There, Jan. 21 2009. Web. 1 Feb. 2009.
(If no author name is specified then simply omit it)

Citing a journal article in print

Format:

Author last name, Author first name. "Article Title." *Journal Name* Volume Number (Year Published): Page Numbers. Medium.

Example:

Gupta, Hanseng. "Studies in how to win." *Winning Science* 12 (2009): 78-93. Print.

Citing a film/Citing a movie
Format:
Film title. Dir. First Name Last Name. Distributor, Year of Release. Medium.
Example:
Bite me. Dir. Albert Schweitzer. Crumptown, 2009. Film.

Citing an encyclopedia entry in print
Format:
Author last name, Author first name. "Article title." *Encyclopedia/Dictionary name*. Year Published. Medium.
Example:
Hansford, Gloria. "Interest." *Encyclopedia Galactica*. 2009. Print.

The Chicago Manual of Style

Bibliography

Citing a book in print
Format:
Author last name, Author first name. *Title of Book*. Publisher City: Publisher Name, Year Published.
Example:
Drown, Bernard. *The Fat Code*. New York: Scholasticalia, 2004.

Citing a magazine article in print
Format:
Author last name, Author first name. *Article title*. Magazine Title, Month Date, Year of publication.
Example:
Ching, James. *The art of mooting*. Moot Magazine, Nov 10, 1985.

Citing a newspaper article in print
Format:
Author last name, Author first name. "Article Title." *Newspaper Name*, Publication Date.

Example:
Gorbachev, Sonia. "Why we'll never win." *Lansing Gazette*, February 2, 2009.

Citing a general website article with an author
Format:
Author last name, Author first name. "Page Title." Website Title. Web Address (retrieved Date Accessed).
Example:
Raygun, Nancy. "Stormin' Norman." CDG.com. http://www.gdg.com/POLITICS/01/21/ Stormin-Norman /index.html (accessed February 1, 2009).

Citing a journal article in print
Format:
Author last name, Author first name. "Article Title." *Journal Name* Volume Number (Year Published): Page Numbers.
Example:
Jones, Amelia. "Studies in Pop Wenderluc." *Weird Nestlings* 12 (2009): 78-93.

Citing a film/Citing a movie
Format:
Film Title. Format. Directed/Performed by First Name Last Name. Original Release Year. Distributor City: Studio/Distributor, Year of Release.
Example:
White War Tomes. DVD. directed by John Dunce. 1999. Los Angeles: Crimea Productions, 2001.

Citing an encyclopedia entry in print
Format:
Author last name, Author first name. *Encyclopedia/Dictionary name*, Edition ed., s.v. "Article Title." Publication City: Publisher Name, Year Published.
Example:
Jones, John. *Encyclopaedia Galactica*, 8th ed., s.v. "Peace." Chicago: Golantosphere, 2009.

10. Review and Edit

It is important to leave yourself enough time to review and edit your essay before submitting it to the teacher for grading. This will help you eradicate typos, change any infelicities or gaffs in writing style and ensure that you have not missed any of the key points that you wanted to make.

There are a number of general issues involved in writing your essay, including your writing style, getting the paragraphing right and some common grammatical and punctuation errors. These are covered in chapter 5 and you should read through that chapter before embarking on your essay.

Chapter 5 – General Points

Here are some general points to note when writing an essay and some practical advice about the nitty gritty of working with word-processing files.

Back up your work

How galling and demoralizing it would be to have just put the finishing touches to your essay's conclusion when you suddenly tip a cup of coffee over your laptop and fry the hard disk. If you think it will never happen to you, then think again. It has happened to even the most careful of users. It is the sort of disaster that only needs to happen to you once for you to lose days' worth of work.

If you are using Microsoft Word, then the first thing you need to do is go into your preferences and set the "Save AutoRecovery info every" option to "1 minute." What this means is that if the program crashes you will be able to recover almost all of your work. After a crash, the first time you open the MS Word program again you will be presented with the most up-to-date version of the file, which should contain everything up to the last minute you were working on it, or more.

However, if your computer gives up the ghost completely, as in the case of the cup of coffee, it is wise to have an external back up just in case. It helps to have an external hard drive attached to your computer, which will back up any new or changed files regularly. This means that, if your computer dies, you can find another computer and load your files onto that.

Worse still, if your cup of coffee fries your external hard drive too (because, after all, there it is sitting on the desk right beside your laptop!) you also need to have a back-up plan for that scenario. There are many different ways of backing up to the Cloud and by the time you read this they may well be superseded, but currently Dropbox is a program that automatically backs up your work to the Internet every time you save your file and there are other facilities such as Evernote and Google Drive, which perform a similar level of backup. This means that if your computer is stolen, damaged or destroyed, you can get most of your files back by downloading the back-up version from the Internet.

Paragraphing

As you go through the body of your essay you will want to divide up the text into paragraphs. A simple rule is, "one idea, one paragraph." In other words, each paragraph should put forward only one idea and should have a single focus. Don't start to wander as you write your paragraph, but keep to the point. Similarly, don't begin your paragraph by talking about one thing and end by talking about something different.

Somewhere in the paragraph it is helpful to include a "topic sentence." A topic sentence is a sentence that summarizes the point you are making in the paragraph. It is also useful to have that sentence right at the start of the paragraph and then go on to provide evidence supporting that statement (including any opposing views which you then demolish).

Some techniques to use when formulating a paragraph:

- Use examples.
- Cite data (facts, statistics, evidence, details, and types of data).
- Examine testimony (what other people say, such as quotes and paraphrases).
- Use an anecdote or story.
- Define terms in the paragraph.
- Compare and contrast.
- Evaluate causes and reasons.
- Examine effects and consequences.
- Analyze the topic.
- Describe the topic.
- Offer the chronology of an event (time segments).

Transitions: Remember to use transitioning words at the beginning of each paragraph if appropriate. Transitional words may be: "In addition to…," "While on the subject of…," "Another factor that plays into this is…."

This is where a lot of essays fall down. The reader needs to know (if not at the beginning, then at least at the end of a paragraph or section), why you are now saying what you are saying. In other words, the points you are making in the essay should not look like a bunch of unrelated statements. True, each paragraph should contain only one point, but the essay should follow a logical course, where one paragraph or point leads to the next, and so on. You are not listing bullet points, but putting forward a logical argument, giving a description, explaining something, or telling a story, depending on the type of essay you have been assigned.

Headings: As you write the essay it may become obvious to you that the topic is divided into two or more discrete subtopics. If that is the case and your essay is long enough it may be a good idea to plant a few headings and/or subheadings in the text and organize the essay around them. This helps the reader to understand what your essay is doing and where it is going, and it may also help to focus your thoughts on the subject better.

Flow

Read each paragraph in the main body of the essay. As mentioned, you should make sure that there is a logical progression from one paragraph to the next. This can be achieved by, for example, structuring the essay as a list of issues which will be covered and enumerating them thus: "First…," "Second…," "Third…," and so on, as you go through the paragraphs. Or you may work from more general points to more specific points as you work your way through the essay. Similarly, you may wish to deal with points chronologically instead, progressing from the past to the present. All that is required is that nothing in your progression of thought jars with the reader as being out of place or forced.

Writing Style

Try to exclude any extraneous words that are not contributing to the argument you are trying to make. Don't waffle, get to the point, and opt for shorter sentences where possible. This will give your writing more of a punch and make it easier for readers to follow what you are saying.

Try to vary the words that you use. Many writers have favorite phrases or words that they use repeatedly. If you are reading through your essay once you have finished the first draft, look out for these kinds of repetition and try to substitute the word or phrase in question with something else.

Try also to vary the opening words of each sentence. If your sentences are all structured in the same way, it makes it difficult for readers to stagger to the end of the essay without falling asleep.

Your essay should be written in a relatively formal style. You should avoid using in-group jargon unless you explain it to the reader first. Slang words and phrases should not be used in a formal essay, unless there is a specific justifiable purpose for it, such as if it is used ironically. Also, avoid using euphemisms to mask more straightforward words or expressions. And lastly avoid using biased language, for example, words that show a racial, gender, ethnic, or group bias or preference.

In general you should try to use active rather than passive sentences. An example of a passive sentence is: *World War II was started by Adolf Hitler*. Its active equivalent would be: *Adolf Hitler started World War II.* Active sentences make your writing much more immediate, readable and engaging. Excessive use of passive sentences can make your writing a little turgid and stuffy. The only exception to this is if you are writing a scientific essay, for example describing an experiment. Then it is more common and acceptable to use the passive voice.

Grammar and Punctuation

Correct grammar and punctuation are important if you want to earn the highest grade for your essay. It is unlikely that you will fail because of poor grammar and punctuation alone (unless you are really abysmal at it). But you could be lowering your grade unnecessarily by not attending to these matters as part of your review of the essay before submitting it to the teacher. Here is a list of the most common grammar and punctuation mistakes and how to fix them. This list is taken from Strunk and White's classic book The Elements of Style and from A Writer's Reference with 2009 MLA and 2010 APA Updates by Diana Hacker.[1]

1. To join two independent clauses, use a comma followed by a conjunction, a semicolon alone, or a semicolon followed by a sentence modifier.

Examples

Incorrect: The delivery boy knew he carried strange cargo, but still ventured off unafraid.
Correct: The delivery boy knew he carried strange cargo, but he still ventured off unafraid.

Incorrect: My math teacher doesn't know how to lecture, she should have remained a student.
Correct: My math teacher doesn't know how to lecture; she should have remained a student.

---

[1] Hacker, Diana. "11 Rules of Writing, Grammar, and Punctuation." Simple Study Guides. http://junketstudies.com/joomla/index.php/11-rules-of-writing/the-rules (May 13, 2016).

Incorrect: Gregor has not changed physically; but has given himself an excuse to separate himself from the pain of previous experiences.
Correct: Gregor has not changed physically; however, he has given himself an excuse to hide from the pain of previous experiences.

2. Use commas to enclose nonrestrictive clauses or phrases, which are not essential to the sentence's meaning.

Examples

Incorrect: The bus driver with her ears tuned to the roar decided to take the grumbling bus on a detour across the football field.
Correct: The bus driver, her ears tuned to the roar, decided to take the grumbling bus on a detour across the football field.

Incorrect: My window as dirty as it is reveals the beauty of nature on a snowy morning.
Correct: My window, as dirty as it is, reveals the beauty of nature on a snowy morning.

Incorrect: King and Lucille, his customized black Gibson have electrified audiences all over the world.
Correct: King and Lucille, his customized black Gibson, have electrified audiences all over the world.

3. Do not use commas to bracket phrases that are essential to a sentence's meaning.

Examples

Incorrect: The man, who has too many ties, has too few necks.
Correct: The man who has too many ties has too few necks.

Incorrect: The cats, with six toes, are a unique attraction of the tour of Hemingway's house.
Correct: The cats with six toes are a unique attraction of the tour of Hemingway's house.

4. When beginning a sentence with an introductory phrase or an introductory (dependent) clause, include a comma.

Examples

Incorrect: After buying the five-pound jar of marshmallow spread he set off in search of a bulk portion of peanut butter.
Correct: After buying the five-pound jar of marshmallow spread, he set off in search of a bulk portion of peanut butter.

Incorrect: With this he bestows the responsibility of his own happiness on his mother and father.
Correct: With this, he bestows the responsibility of his own happiness on his mother and father.

Incorrect: As she begins to gain independence it is natural for Grete to regard the idea of dependency as repugnant.
Correct: As she begins to gain independence, it is natural for Grete to regard the idea of dependency as repugnant.

5. To indicate possession, end a singular noun with an apostrophe followed by an "s". Otherwise, the noun's form seems plural.

Examples

Incorrect: Though the lobsters claws were bound, the creature made a threatening gesture as they dropped it in the pot.
Correct: Though the lobster's claws were bound, the creature made a threatening gesture as they dropped it in the pot.

Incorrect: In a democracy, anyones vote counts as much as mine.
Correct: In a democracy, anyone's vote counts as much as mine.

Incorrect: There is a vast age difference between Victors mother and father.
Correct: There is a vast age difference between Victor's mother and father.

6. Use proper punctuation to integrate a quotation into a sentence. If the introductory material is an independent clause, add the quotation after a colon. If the introductory material ends in "thinks," "saying," or

some other verb indicating expression, use a comma.

Examples

Incorrect: Tumbling down the hill, Jack yelled: "Gosh, I'm sick of this."
Correct: Tumbling down the hill, Jack yelled, "Gosh, I'm sick of this."

Incorrect: Her letter spoke to him in harsh tones, "You never fail to repulse me."
Correct: Her letter spoke to him in harsh tones: "You never fail to repulse me."

Incorrect: He views the problem as a slight delay or a sickness that will eventually disappear, "I will go back to sleep for a few minutes and forget all this nonsense."
Correct: He views the problem as a slight delay or a sickness that will eventually disappear: "I will go back to sleep for a few minutes and forget all this nonsense."

7. Make the subject and verb agree with each other, not with a word that comes between them.

Examples

Incorrect: The Thanksgiving dinner, right down to the beautiful centerpiece, were devoured by the escaped grizzly.
Correct: The Thanksgiving dinner, right down to the beautiful centerpiece, was devoured by the escaped grizzly.

Incorrect: The cart, as well as its contents, were gone.
Correct: The cart, as well as its contents, was gone.

Incorrect: The girl, along with her classmates, like the new teacher.
Correct: The girl, along with her classmates, likes the new teacher.

8. Be sure that a pronoun, a participial phrase, or an appositive refers clearly to the proper subject.

Examples

Incorrect: Its hump decorated in strings of flowers, the programmer rode the camel through the food court.
Correct: The programmer rode the camel, its hump decorated in strings of flowers, through the food court.

Incorrect: Filled with bad gas, he drove his car to Tucson despite the knocking.
Correct: Although it was filled with bad gas, he drove his car to Tucson despite the knocking.

9. Use parallel construction to make a strong point and create a smooth flow.

Examples

Incorrect: I was glad to be departing for Australia but I was nervous when I left my apartment.
Correct: I was glad to be departing for Australia but nervous to be leaving my apartment.

Incorrect: The system excels at tasks, such as communicating with other computers, processing records, and mathematical calculations.
Correct: The system excels at tasks such as communicating with other computers, processing records, and calculating mathematical equations.

10. Omit unnecessary words.

Examples

Incorrect: I would like to assert that the author should be considered to be a buffoon.
Correct: The author is a buffoon.

Incorrect: It would be safe to say that Gregor Samsa is not the only character in Franz Kafka's The Metamorphosis to undergo drastic changes.
Correct: Gregor Samsa is not the only character in Franz Kafka's The Metamorphosis to undergo drastic change.

Incorrect: Before going to the supermarket, we made a list of the groceries we needed in order to make the food that we intended to eat for dinner.
Correct: Before going to the supermarket, we made a list of groceries that we needed to prepare dinner.

Seeking Help

No matter how good you are at essay writing, there always remains the possibility that you can get stuck. Is your essay structured properly? Have you run out of things to say? Is your thesis statement too general or unclear? Where do you find background research material? Any of these problems can cause you to run aground and your essay to stall. The first thing to do if you are stuck in this way is to read this book again. Maybe there is something you missed when you read it first time around. But if you've done that but still feel that your essay is not going smoothly, then go to the source, i.e. the teacher / professor / tutor who has set the essay question.

Most teachers are quite happy to make themselves available to discuss how you tackle your essay. On the other hand, if the trouble you are finding is related to your writing style, or how to rescue your essay from the pit of incomprehensibility it has sunk into, your teacher may be able to point you in the direction of someone who can help you get back on track and salvage the good parts of the essay while cutting out the bad. Many universities also have Writing Centers where students can go to get help with essay-writing.

Chapter 6 - Conclusion

Writing essays can seem daunting if you've never done it before, or if you don't really know how to tackle them. But once you can grasp the basics, and with a little practice, the task becomes much more manageable. As with many things, if you break the production of an essay down into smaller steps it seems much less formidable and scary. In this short book, I have endeavored to do just that, taking the essay and simplifying the process into small individual stages that, hopefully, anyone can manage.

The argumentative essay in particular seems to be the type of beast that chills students to the marrow and seems like an impossible obstacle that just can't be moved. The reason for this is probably that many institutions don't really give much guidance in the technique of writing essays, so students are all at sea. I hope this book goes some way to alleviating the onerous burden of essay-writing. Who knows? One day you might even find essay-writing fun!

Sean O'Neill

ABOUT THE AUTHOR

Originally from Scotland, Sean O'Neill has traveled a bit, including living in Ireland, England (twice), Italy and the USA - which is where he currently lives. He worked as a freelance journalist for about seven years in the UK, and had a regular weekly column in national Sunday newspapers. He has had poetry, short stories and articles published in a variety of publications. To date, he has published six books of poetry and two books of light verse. He has also published six novels which range from thigh-slappingly funny, to nail-bitingly tense, and every possible nuance in between, along with five non-fiction books on the art and practice of writing and publishing. All of his books are available on Amazon and other online book retailers. When he is not publishing books, Sean O'Neill works as a translator and has translated numerous books into English.

CPSIA information can be obtained
at www.ICGtesting.com
Printed in the USA
FSHW012231031021
85204FS